Introduction

Whether your only knitting experience has been making a scarf or you've been making sweaters for everyone you know, you'll enjoy this selection of fashionable knit ponchos.

They're designed with an understanding of stitch patterns, yarns and how a knitted fabric drapes on a body. All seven designs are fun to knit and will work up quickly. After all, most ponchos are really only two rectangles that are then sewn together. Really, no more difficult than knitting a scarf!

Contents

Instructions

Brush Strokes

Skill Level

EASY

Sizes

Small/medium, large/extra-large

Chest measurement: 32 inches–38 inches, 40 inches–46 inches

Note: Instructions are written for size small/medium; changes for large/extra-large are in parentheses.

Materials

Bulky (chunky) weight yarn, 5 oz (230 yds, 140g) variegated

Note: Our photographed poncho was made with Lion Brand Jiffy, country evening #359.

Size 15 (10mm) knitting needles

Size 17 (12.75mm) knitting needles or size needed to obtain gauge

Size 13 tapestry needle

Gauge

With larger needles in pat st:

2 sts = 1 inch

Instructions

Side Panel (make 2)
With smaller needles, cast on 59 (65) sts.

Row 1 (WS):
P1; *k1; p1; rep from * across.

Row 2 (RS):
K1; *p1; k1; rep from * across.

Rows 3 and 4:
Rep Rows 1 and 2 once more.

Row 5:
Rep Row 1.

Change to larger needles.

Row 6:
Knit.

Row 7:
P1; *yo, p2tog; rep from * across.

Rep Row 7 until piece measures approx 10 (9½) inches, ending by working a RS row.

Change to smaller needles.

Next row:
Rep Row 7.

Next row:
Knit.

Next 4 rows:
Rep Rows 1 and 2 twice.

Bind off in pat.

Finishing
Step 1:
Block pieces to measure 29 x 12 inches (32 x 11½ inches). *(Note: Ribbing sections should be slightly stretched to maintain rectangular shape of pieces.)*

Seam

Step 2:
Referring to diagram, sew pieces tog.

Floating Coasters

Instructions

Side Panel (make 2)
With larger needles, cast on 74 (82) sts.

Row 1 (WS):
P1; *yo, p4tog; rep from * to last st; p1. 38 (42) sts

Row 2 (RS):
K2; *in next st work (k1, yo, k1); k1; rep from * across. 74 (82) sts

Row 3:
P1; *p4tog, yo; rep from * to last st; p1. 38 (42) sts

Row 4:
K1; *in next st work (k1, yo, k1); k1; rep from * to last st; k1. 74 (82) sts

Rows 5 through 28:
Rep Rows 1 through 4 six times more.

Change to smaller needles.

Row 29:
P1; *yo, p2tog twice; rep from * to last st; p1. 56 (62) sts

Rows 30 through 35:
Knit.

Bind off.

Finishing
Step 1:
Block pieces to measure 25 x 11 inches (28 x 11 inches).

Step 2:
Referring to diagram, sew pieces tog.

Skill Level

EASY

Sizes
Small/medium, large/extra-large

Chest measurement: 32 inches–38 inches, 40 inches–46 inches

Note: Instructions are written for size small/medium; changes for large/extra-large are in parentheses.

Materials

Bulky (chunky) weight yarn, 5 oz (167 yds, 113g) variegated

Note: Our photographed poncho was made with Lion Brand Color Waves, caribbean #307.

Size 13 (9mm) knitting needles

Size 15 (10mm) knitting needles or size required for gauge

Tapestry needle

Gauge
With larger needles in pat st:

4 rep = 5½ inches

8 rows = 2½ inches

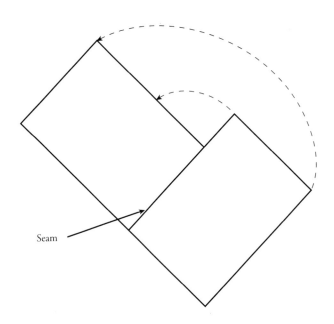

Seam

Yin & Yang

Skill Level

EASY

Sizes

Small/medium, large/extra-large

Chest measurement: 32 inches–38 inches,
   40 inches–46 inches

Note: Instructions are written for size small/medium; changes for large/extra-large are in parentheses.

Materials

Medium (worsted) weight yarn, 3 oz (120 yds, 90g) each, orange and blue

Note: Our photographed poncho was made with Lion Brand Cotton-Ease, orangeade #133 and candy blue #107.

Size 10.5 (6.5mm) knitting needles or size required for gauge

Tapestry needle

Gauge

In pat st:

3 sts = 1 inch

Pattern Stitch
Openwork Pattern

Row 1 (WS):
K1, purl to last st; k1.

Row 2 (RS):
K1, *k2tog, yo; rep from * to last 2 sts; k2.

Row 3:
K1, purl to last st; k1.

Row 4:
K2; *yo, ssk; rep from * to last st; k1.

Instructions

First Side Panel

With orange, cast on 71 (79) sts.

Rep Rows 1 through 4 of Openwork Pattern in following color sequence:

3 rows orange

2 rows blue

6 rows orange

2 rows blue

6 rows orange

2 rows blue

3 rows orange

Continuing as established, rep Rows 1 through 4 until piece measures approx 8½ (9) inches, ending by working a Row 1 or 3.

Next 2 rows:
Knit.
Bind off.

Second Side Panel

With blue, cast on 71 (79) sts.

Rep Rows 1 through 4 of Openwork Pattern in following color sequence:

3 rows blue

2 rows orange

6 rows blue

2 rows orange

6 rows blue

2 rows orange

3 rows blue

Continuing as established, rep Rows 1 through 4 until piece measures approx 8½ (9) inches, ending by working a Row 1 or 3.

Next 2 rows:
Knit.
Bind off.

Finishing

Step 1:
Block pieces to measure 24 x 9 inches (26 x 9½ inches).

Step 2:
Referring to diagram, sew pieces tog.

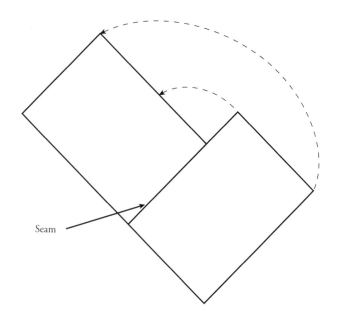

Seam

Honeycomb Lace

Size

Small/medium, large/extra-large

Chest measurement: 32 inches–38 inches,
    40 inches–46 inches

Note: *Instructions are written for size small/medium; changes for large/extra-large are in parentheses.*

Materials

Fine (sport) weight yarn, 5 oz (435 yds, 140g) off-white

Note: *Our photographed poncho was made with Lion Brand Wool-Ease Sport weight, fisherman #099.*

Size 8 (5mm) knitting needles or size required for gauge

Tapestry needle

Gauge

In main pat st:

5 sts = 1 inch

Special Abbreviation

C4B (Cable 4 Back)

Sl 2 sts onto cn and hold in back; k2; knit 2 sts from cn.

Instructions

Side Panel (make 2)

Cast on 51 sts.

Row 1 (WS):
K1; p4; k46.

Row 2 (RS):
K45; p1; C4B; p1.

Row 3:
K1, p4, k1; *k2tog; yo twice; k2tog; rep from * to last st; k1.

Row 4:
K2; *in double yo work (k1, p1); k2; rep from * 9 times more; k1, p1 in double yo; k1; p1; k4; p1.

Row 5:
K1; p4; k1; *yo; k2tog twice; yo; rep from * to last st; k1.

Row 6:
K4; *in double yo work (k1, p1); k2; rep from * 9 times more; k1; p1; C4B; p1.

Rep Rows 3 through 6 until piece measures approx 20 inches (21½ inches), ending by working Row 6.

Next row:
K1, p4, k46.

Bind off as follows: K45, k2tog, k1, k2tog, k1.

Finishing

Step 1:
Block pieces to measure 20½ x 9 inches (22 x 9 inches).

Step 2:
Referring to diagram, sew pieces tog with cable edge at neckline.

Step 3:
Following Fringe instructions on page 15, make Single Knot Fringe. Cut 4-inch strands; use 4 strands for each knot. Tie knots through every other st across cast-on edges, through each yo across side edges, and at each V. Trim ends even.

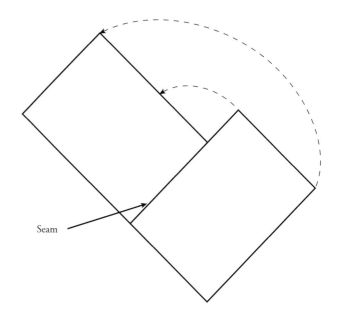

Seam

Posh

Skill Level

EASY

Sizes

Small/medium, large/extra-large

Chest measurement: 32 inches–38 inches,
40 inches–46 inches

Note: *Instructions are written for size small/medium; changes for large/extra-large are in parentheses.*

Materials

Bulky (chunky) weight yarn, 5 1/2 (6 1/4) oz /224 (254) yds /157 (179)g blue

Novelty fur yarn, 2 (2 1/4) oz /88 (99) yds /57 (64)g blue and brown variegated

Note: *Our photographed poncho was made with Patons Divine, halo blue #06106, and Patons Cha Cha, hippie, #02007.*

Size 13 (9mm) circular knitting needle

Size 15 (10mm) circular knitting needle

Size 17 (12.75) circular needle or size required for gauge

Size 13 tapestry needle

One blue button, 1 1/4-inch

Sewing needle and matching thread

Gauge

With largest needle in pat st with one strand bulky yarn:
5 sts = 3 inches

Pattern Note

Circular needle is used to accommodate large number of sts; work back and forth in rows. Do not join.

Instructions

Note: *Slip sts as to knit.*

With largest needle and two strands novelty fur yarn, cast on 87 (99) sts.

Rows 1 through 5:
Knit.

Cut novelty fur yarn; join one strand bulky yarn.

Row 6 (RS):
Knit.

Row 7:
K1; purl to last st; k1.

Row 8:
K3; *yo, sl 1, k2tog, psso; yo, k3; rep from * 13 (15) times more.

Row 9:
Rep Row 7.

Row 10:
K1, k2tog; yo; *k3, yo, sl 1, k2tog, psso; yo; rep from * 12 (14) times more; yo, k3, yo, ssk; k1.

Rep Rows 7 through 10 until piece measures approx 16 (17) inches, ending by working a Row 8 or 10.

Note: *When measuring, be sure piece is flat and not stretched, as this pattern tends to grow vertically and shrink horizontally.*

Change to medium size needle.

Continue in pat until piece measures approx 19 (20) inches, ending by working a Row 8 or 10.

Change to smallest needle.

Continue in pat until piece measures approx 22 (23) inches, ending by working a Row 7 or 9.

Next row:
K1; purl to last st; k1.

Bind off purlwise.

Finishing
Step 1:
Block piece to measure 52 x 22 1/2 inches (59 x 23 1/2 inches).

Step 2:
Lay piece with WS facing you. Fold right-hand edge and left-hand edge to meet at center. Sew upper right-hand corner over upper left-hand corner at 45 degree angle, overlapping 2 (2 1/2) inches at neck edge.

Step 3:
Sew button through all layers of closure.

Skill Level

■ ■ ☐ ☐

EASY

Sizes

Small/medium, large/extra-large

Chest measurement: 32 inches–38 inches,
40 inches–46 inches

Note: *Instructions are written for size small/medium; changes for large/extra-large are in parentheses.*

Materials

Medium (worsted) weight glitter yarn, 10½ (13) oz/690 (854) yds/300 (372)g bronze

Note: *Our photographed poncho was made with Lion Brand Glitterspun, bronze #135.*

Size 11 (8mm) circular knitting needle

Size 15 (10mm) circular knitting needle or size required for gauge

Tapestry needle

One black button, ¾-inch

Sewing needle and matching thread

Gauge

With larger needle in pat:

7 sts = 2 inches unblocked

Pattern Note

Circular needle is used to accommodate large number of sts; work back and forth in rows. Do not join.

Instructions

With larger needle, cast on 146 (178) sts.

Row 1 (WS):
P1; *p3tog; in next st work (k1, p1, k1); rep from * to last st; p1.

Row 2 (RS):
Purl.

Row 3:
P1; *in next st work (k1, p1, k1); p3tog; rep from * to last st; p1.

Row 4:
Purl.

Rep Rows 1 through 4 until piece measures approx 16 (17) inches, ending by working a Row 2.

Note: *When measuring, be sure piece is flat and not stretched, as this pattern tends to grow vertically and shrink horizontally.*

Change to smaller needles.

Neck Shaping

Row 1:
P1, [in next st work (k1, p1, k1); p3tog] 9 (10) times; *in next st work (k1, p1, k1); p3tog; p1; p3tog; in next st work (k1, p1, k1); p3tog; rep from * 5 (7) times more; [in next st work (k1, p1, k1); p3tog] 9 (10) times; p1. 134 (162) sts

Row 2:
Purl.

Row 3:
P39 (43); *p2tog; p3; rep from * 11 (15) times more; p35 (39). 122 (146) sts

Row 4:
Purl.

Row 5:
P37 (41); *p2tog; p2; rep from * 11 (15) times more; p37 (41). 110 (130) sts

Row 6:
Purl.

Bind off as follows: P38 (42); *p2tog; p1; rep from * 11 (15) times more; p36 (40).

Finishing

Step 1:
Block piece to measure 38 x 19 inches (46 x 20 inches).

Step 2:
Following Fringe instructions on page 15, make Triple Knot Fringe. Cut 18-inch strands of yarn; use 4 strands for each knot. Tie 1 knot through every 4th st across bottom edge and every 5th row across side edges, and 2 knots in each corner. On 3rd row of knots, do not tie a knot on either end of fringe.

Step 3:
Lay piece flat with WS facing you; fold right-hand edge over to meet left-hand edge. Sew upper left back corner over upper left front corner, overlapping 2 (2½) inches at neck edge and having tip of back corner 1 inch from side edge.

Step 4:
Sew button through all layers of corner closure.

Skill Level

EASY

Sizes

Small/medium, large/extra-large

Chest measurement: 32 inches–38 inches,
    40 inches–46 inches

Note: *Instructions are written for size small/medium; changes for large/extra-large are in parentheses.*

Materials

Bulky (chunky) weight yarn, 15 (15½) oz /608 (628) yds/429 (443)g pink

Note: *Our photographed poncho was made with Patons Divine, chantilly rose #06406.*

Size 17 (12.75) circular needle or size required for gauge

Tapestry needle

Gauge

In pat stitch:

11 sts = 6 inches

Pattern Note

Circular needle is used to accommodate large number of sts; work back and forth in rows. Do not join.

Instructions

Front/Back Panel (make 2)

Cast on 81 (85) sts.

Row 1 (RS):
Purl.

Row 2:
Knit.

Row 3:
P5 (7); *yo, p2tog, p8; rep from * 6 times more; yo, p2tog; p4 (6).

Row 4:
Knit.

Row 5:
P3 (5); *p2tog, yo, p1, yo, p2tog, p5; rep from * 6 times more; p2tog, yo, p1, yo, p2tog; p3 (5).

Row 6:
Knit.

Row 7:
P4 (6); *p2tog, yo p8; rep from * 6 times more; p2tog, yo p5 (7).

Row 8:
Knit.

Row 9:
Purl.

Row 10:
Knit.

Row 11:
P10 (12); *yo, p2tog, p8; rep from * 6 times more; p1 (3).

Row 12:
Knit.

Row 13:
P8 (10); *p2tog, yo, p1, yo, p2tog, p5; rep from * 6 times more; p3 (5).

Row 14:
Knit.

Row 15:
P9 (11); *p2tog, yo, p8; rep from * 6 times more; p2 (4).

Row 16:
Knit.

Rep Rows 1 through 16 until piece measures approx 22 (23) inches, ending by working a knit row.

Bind off purlwise.

Finishing

Step 1:
Block pieces to measure 44 x 22 inches (46 x 23 inches).

Step 2:
Sew bound-off edges of panels tog for shoulder seams, leaving center 12 (13) inches open for neck.

Step 3:
Following Fringe instructions on page 15, make Single Knot Fringe. Cut 6-inch strands; use 2 strands for each knot.
Tie knots through every other st across arm edges. Trim ends even.

Abbreviations & Symbols

beg	begin(ning)		sl st(s)	slip stitch(es)
BL(s)	back loop(s)		sp(s)	space(s)
ch(s)	chain(s)		st(s)	stitch(es)
dc	double crochet(s)		tog	together
dec	decrease(ing)		yd(s)	yard(s)
g	gram(s)		YO	yarn over
K	knit			
K2tog	knit 2 together			
lp(s)	loop(s)			
oz	ounce(s)			
P	purl			
P2 tog	purl 2 together			
pat	pattern			
prev	previous			
PSSO	pass slipped stitch over			
rem	remain(ing)			
rep	repeat(ing)			
sc	single crochet(s)			
sk	skip			
sl	slip			

* An asterisk is used to mark the beginning of a portion of instructions to be worked more than once; thus, "rep from * twice more" means after working the instructions once, repeat the instructions following the asterisk twice more (three times in all).

† The dagger identifies a portion of instructions that will be repeated again later in the same row or round.

() Parentheses are used to enclose instructions that should be worked the exact number of times specified immediately following the parentheses, such as "(2 sc in next dc, sc in next dc) twice." They are also used to set off and clarify a group of stitches that are to be worked all into the same space or stitch, such as "in next corner sp work (2 dc, ch 1, 2 dc)."

[] Brackets and **()** parentheses are used to provide additional information to clarify instructions.

Join—join with a sl st unless otherwise specified.

How to Check Gauge

A correct stitch gauge is very important. Please take the time to work a stitch gauge swatch about 4 x 4 inches. Measure the swatch. If the number of stitches and rows are fewer than indicated under "Gauge" in the pattern, your needle is too large. Try another swatch with a smaller size hook. If the number of stitches and rows are more than indicated under "Gauge" in the pattern, your needle is too small. Try another swatch with a larger size hook.

Fringe

Basic Instructions

Cut a piece of cardboard half as long as specified in instructions for strands plus ½ inch for trimming allowance. Wind yarn loosely and evenly lengthwise around cardboard. When card is filled, cut yarn across one end. Do this several times, then begin fringing; you can wind additional strands as you need them.

Single Knot Fringe

Hold specified number of strands for one knot of fringe together, then fold in half. Hold scarf with right side facing you. Use crochet hook to draw folded end through space or stitch from right to wrong side (**Figs 1** and **2**), pull loose ends through folded section (**Fig 3**) and draw knot up firmly (**Fig 4**). Space knots as indicated in pattern instructions.

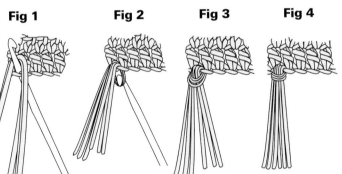

Fig 1 **Fig 2** **Fig 3** **Fig 4**

Double Knot Fringe

Begin by working Single Knot Fringe completely across one end of scarf. With right side facing you and working from left to right, take half the strands of one knot and half the strands in the knot next to it, and knot them together (**Fig 5**).

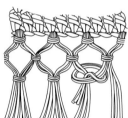

Triple Knot Fringe

First work Double Knot Fringe. Then working again on the right side from left to right, tie third row of knots as in **Fig 6**.

Fig 6

Skill Levels

BEGINNER
Beginner projects for first-time knitters and crocheters using basic stitches. Minimal shaping.

EASY
Easy projects using basic stitches, repetitive stitch patterns, simple color changes and simple shaping and finishing.

INTERMEDIATE
Intermediate projects with a variety of stitches, mid-level shaping and finishing.

EXPERIENCED
Experienced projects using advanced techniques and stitches, detailed shaping and refined finishing.

Metric Charts

KNITTING NEEDLE CONVERSION CHART

U.S.	1	2	3	4	5	6	7	8	9	10	10½	11	13	15	17	19	35	50
Continental-mm	2.25	2.75	3.25	3.5	3.75	4	4.5	5	5.5	6	6.5	8	9	10	12.75	15	19	25

Standard Yarn Weight System

Categories of yarn, gauge ranges, and recommended needle and hook sizes

Yarn Weight Symbol & Category Names	1 SUPER FINE	2 FINE	3 LIGHT	4 MEDIUM	5 BULKY	6 SUPER BULKY
Type of Yarns in Category	Sock, Fingering, Baby	Sport, Baby	DK, Light Worsted	Worsted, Afghan, Aran	Chunky, Craft, Rug	Bulky, Roving
Knit Gauge Range* in Stockinette Stitch to 4 inches	27–32 sts	23–26 sts	21–24 sts	16–20 sts	12–15 sts	6–11 sts
Recommended Needle in Metric Size Range	2.25–3.25 mm	3.25–3.75 mm	3.75–4.5 mm	4.5–5.5 mm	5.5–8 mm	8 mm and larger
Recommended Needle U.S. Size Range	1 to 3	3 to 5	5 to 7	7 to 9	9 to 11	11 and larger
Crochet Gauge* Ranges in Single Crochet to 4 inch	21–32 sts	16–20 sts	12–17 sts	11–14 sts	8–11 sts	5–9 sts
Recommended Hook in Metric Size Range	2.25–3.5 mm	3.5–4.5 mm	4.5–5.5 mm	5.5–6.5 mm	6.5–9 mm	9 mm and larger
Recommended Hook U.S. Size Range	B1–E4	E4–7	7–I9	I-9–K-10½	K-10½–M-13	M-13 and larger

* GUIDELINES ONLY: The above reflect the most commonly used gauges and needle or hook sizes for specific yarn categories.

American School of Needlework®
excellence in instruction

DRG Publishing
306 East Parr Road
Berne, IN 46711

©2004 American School of Needlework
TOLL-FREE ORDER LINE or to request a free catalog (800) 582-6643
Customer Service (800) 282-6643, **Fax** (800) 882-6643

Visit www.AnniesAttic.com.